"You are never too small to make a difference."

—Greta Thunberg

OUR H
ON

Jeanette Winter

OUSE IS

Greta Thunberg's Call to Save the Planet

FIRE

BEACH LANE BOOKS NEW YORK LONDON TORONTO SYDNEY NEW DELHI

Greta is a quiet girl who led a quiet life
in the city of Stockholm.
Her dog Roxy was her friend.

"All my life I've been invisible . . .

. . . the invisible girl in the back who doesn't say anything."
In school she felt alone.

Then one day Greta's teacher talked to the class about the climate, about
how our planet is getting warmer, about how the polar ice is melting,
about how animals' lives are threatened.
And ours, too.

That's when Greta's life changed.
She read for hours and watched film after film
about our warming world.

Greta could think about one thing for a long, long time.

She saw ice melting into the sea, disappearing.

She saw mighty winds and torrential rains
howling across the land.

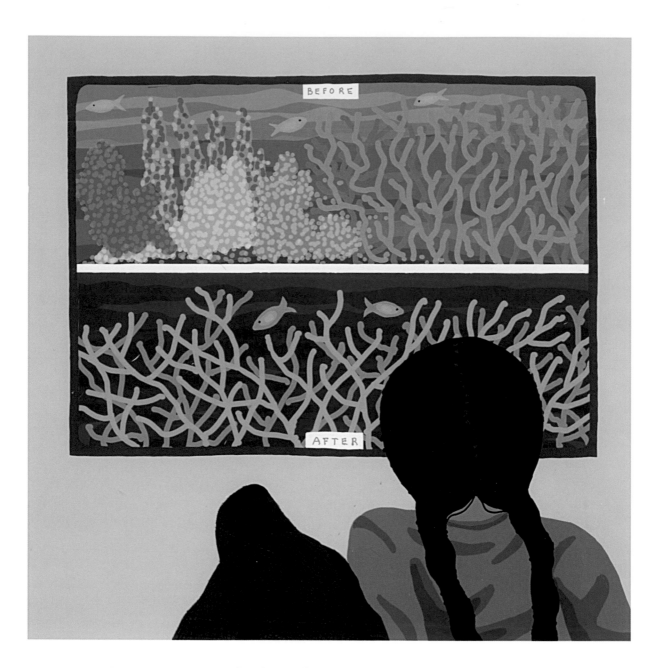

She saw coral reefs, deep down in the sea, pale as ghosts,
bleached by the warming waters.

Greta saw living creatures everywhere,
struggling to stay alive.

Greta saw floodwaters covering houses
and people and animals.

She saw cities swallowed under rising oceans.

She saw the smoldering sun scorch the earth,
leaving it bone-dry.

She saw blazing wildfires, racing through the forests.

OUR HOUSE IS ON FIRE

Greta became sad, thinking about the climate all the time.
She barely ate or spoke.

"Those pictures were stuck in my mind."

The sad days went on for a long time,
each day more unhappy than the next.
There might not be a world to live in when she grows up.
What use is school without a future?
What can I do, she wondered.

Greta decided to go on strike from school—for the climate.

Her parents understood.

Greta skipped school one Friday and took her poster—
SCHOOL STRIKE FOR CLIMATE—
to the Parliament building to sit on strike.
She hoped lawmakers would see her.

People walked past, too busy to notice.
Greta was invisible there, too.

She was at the Parliament building every Friday,
even in the rain.

Then word of her strike began to spread.
Little by little, other school strikers joined her.
On Fridays, Stockholm schools were a bit empty.

More people started noticing the child strikers,
and word spread through cyberspace about the Friday school strikes.

Children started striking everywhere.
If grown-ups won't act to save the planet, children will.

The quiet girl who always felt invisible was asked to speak to very important people at the United Nations climate talks in Poland.

Greta only spoke when she thought it was necessary.

"You say you love your children above all else, and yet you are stealing their future in front of their very eyes."

"We need to keep the fossil fuels in the ground."

The quiet girl was invited to speak to important people
at the World Economic Forum in Davos, Switzerland.
It was necessary to speak.

"I don't want you to be hopeful.

I want you to panic.

I want you to feel the fear
I feel every day. . . .

I want you to act as if
the house was on fire.

Because it is."

Greta's protest, all alone, sparked a worldwide children's march.
Her quiet voice, joined by thousands of voices, became a roar.

CAN YOU
HEAR
US?

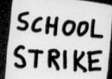

Greta Thunberg was fifteen years old when she first skipped school one Friday to strike for climate change in front of the Swedish Parliament building in Stockholm. Her lone call to action on August 20, 2018, sparked a children's movement that led to Friday school strikes in many countries and culminated in a worldwide Friday march on March 15, 2019.

Among the countries where students marched were:

Argentina	Colombia	Finland	Ireland	Mexico	Portugal	Spain	United States
Australia	Croatia	France	Italy	Netherlands	Russia	Sweden	Uruguay
Austria	Cyprus	Germany	Japan	New Zealand	Slovakia	Switzerland	
Belgium	China	Greece	Latvia	Norway	Slovenia	Thailand	
Canada	Czech Republic	Iceland	Luxembourg	Philippines	South Africa	Ukraine	
Chile	Denmark	India	Malta	Poland	South Korea	United Kingdom	

Sources

Gessen, Masha. "The Fifteen-Year-Old Climate Activist Who Is Demanding a New Kind of Politics." *The New Yorker*, October 2, 2018, www.newyorker.com/news/our-columnists/the-fifteen-year-old-climate-activist-who-is-demanding-a-new-kind-of-politics.

"Greta Thunberg Full Speech at UN Climate Change COP24 Conference." Speech by Greta Thunberg, *YouTube*, Connect4Climate, December 15, 2018, www.youtube.com/watch?v=VFkQSGyeCWg.

"Greta Thunberg Speech to UN Secretary General António Guterres." Speech by Greta Thunberg, *YouTube*, Fridays4Future, December 4, 2018, www.youtube.com/watch?v=Hq489387cg4.

"Greta Thunberg 'Our House Is on Fire' 2019 World Economic Forum (WEF) in Davos." Speech by Greta Thunberg, *YouTube*, UPFSI, January 25, 2019, www.youtube.com/watch?v=zrF1THd4bUM.

Hook, Leslie. "Greta Thunberg: 'All My Life I've Been the Invisible Girl.'" *Financial Times*, February 22, 2019, www.ft.com/content/4df1b9e6-34fb-11e9-bd3a-8b2a211d90d5.

"School Strike for Climate—Save the World by Changing the Rules." Speech by Greta Thunberg, *YouTube*, TedxStockholm, December 12, 2018, www.youtube.com/watch?v=EAmmUIEsN9A.

Sengupta, Somini. "Becoming Greta: 'Invisible Girl' to Global Climate Activist, with Bumps Along the Way." *New York Times*, February 18, 2019, www.nytimes.com/2019/02/18/climate/greta-thunburg.html.

Watts, Jonathan. "'The Beginning of Great Change': Greta Thunberg Hails School Climate Strikes." *The Guardian*, February 15, 2019, www.theguardian.com/environment/2019/feb/15/the-beginning-of-great-change-greta-thunberg-hails-school-climate-strikes.

"You Are Stealing Our Future: Greta Thunberg, 15, Condemns the World's Inaction on Climate Change." Report by Amy Goodman, *Daily Show*, Democracy Now!, December 13, 2018, www.democracynow.org/shows/2018/12/13.

Quotes

"You are never too small to make a difference." [Quote from COP24 Poland speech]

"All my life I've been invisible, the invisible girl in the back who doesn't say anything." [Quoted by Leslie Hook, *Financial Times*]

"Those pictures were stuck in my head." [Quoted by Jonathan Watts, *Guardian*]

"You say you love your children above all else, and yet you are stealing their future in front of their very eyes." [Quote from COP24 Poland speech]

"We need to keep the fossil fuels in the ground." [Quote from COP24 Poland speech]

"I don't want you to be hopeful. I want you to panic. I want you to feel the fear I feel every day. . . . I want you to act as if the house was on fire. Because it is." [Quote from World Economic Forum (WEF) speech in Davos]

When I heard her speeches, I felt Greta was speaking for me. And I'm eighty years old.
—Jeanette Winter

BEACH LANE BOOKS • An imprint of Simon & Schuster Children's Publishing Division • 1230 Avenue of the Americas, New York, New York 10020 • Copyright © 2019 by Jeanette Winter • All rights reserved, including the right of reproduction in whole or in part in any form. • BEACH LANE BOOKS is a trademark of Simon & Schuster, Inc. • For information about special discounts for bulk purchases, please contact Simon & Schuster Special Sales at 1-866-506-1949 or business@simonandschuster.com. • The Simon & Schuster Speakers Bureau can bring authors to your live event. For more information or to book an event, contact the Simon & Schuster Speakers Bureau at 1-866-248-3049 or visit our website at www.simonspeakers.com. • Book design by Irene Metaxatos • The text for this book was set in Encode Sans. • Manufactured in the United States of America • 0919 PHE • First Edition • 10 9 8 7 6 5 4 3 2 1 • Library of Congress Control Number: 2019947458 • ISBN 978-1-5344-6778-1 • ISBN 978-1-5344-6779-8 (eBook)